101 Thoughts of the Day

Sue -
you are a
Masterpiece!
Lisa Collett

101 Thoughts of the Day

LISA COLLETT

Tate Publishing & *Enterprises*

Published by Tate Publishing & Enterprises, LLC
127 E. Trade Center Terrace | Mustang, Oklahoma 73064 USA
1.888.361.9473 | www.tatepublishing.com

Tate Publishing is committed to excellence in the publishing industry. The company reflects the philosophy established by the founders, based on Psalm 68:11,
"The Lord gave the word and great was the company of those who published it."

Cover design by Kenna Davis
Interior design by Chelsea Womble

Published in the United States of America

ISBN: 978-1-61777-420-1
1. Religion, Christian Life, Inspirational
2. Religion, Christian Life, Women's Issues
11.04.29

Dedication

To my husband, Roland, my best friend and the love of my life: I love you with all my heart. I love sharing my life with you. Thank you for believing in me when I share my dreams with you. You are my support team. I am so thankful God gave me a man of faith, who loves the Lord. You are my sweetheart and I love you.

To my dad, Junior: What can I say about a man that molded and shaped my life? Thank you for always praying with me and reading me Bible stories as I was growing up. But most of all, thank you for showing me Jesus. I love you.

To my stepmom, Pat: You have always believed in me, and I cherish that. When I share my thoughts with you, you are always so supportive. You are a true friend. I love you.

This book is dedicated to my mother, Vernita McKinney (1947–2006): Who I am today is because of her blood, sweat, and tears; a true woman of God.

Table of Contents

Day 1

You Are Amazing! You Are Not A Mistake And Someone Needs What Only You Can Give.

> You made all the delicate, inner parts of my body and knit me together in my mother's womb. Thank you for making me so wonderfully complex! Your workmanship is marvelous how well I know it. You watched me as I was being formed in utter seclusion, as I was woven together in the dark of the womb. You saw me before I was born. Every day of my life was recorded in your book. Every moment was laid out before a single day had passed.
>
> Psalm 139:13–16 (NLT)

This passage is a reminder to us that we are not mistakes. Maybe you came as a shock to your parents, but not to God. He made all your delicate, inner parts, and you were formed in utter seclusion. My favorite part of that passage is "Every day of my life was recorded in your book." God made you so amazing that there is not another human like you. God put you together perfectly. He has an assignment for all of us, and your assignment is to reach out and touch other people in the way that only you can. Ask him to use you to reach someone today. You are amazing!

Day 2

This Is A New Day. Choose To Be Happy.

> Taste and see that the Lord is good. Oh, the joy of those who take refuge in him!
>
> Psalm 34:8 (NLT)

> This is the day that the Lord has made. We will rejoice and be glad in it.
>
> Psalm 118:24 (NLT)

There's nothing like a brand new day. You could have had the worst day ever the day before; nothing went right for you, starting with spilling your coffee first thing. After a great night sleep and your feet hit the floor, it's a new day. You can choose what kind of day you are going to have. It's your attitude toward what comes at you that determines what kind of day you will have. Take one day at a time. Life is like climbing a mountain. You take one step at a time; everyone knows two or three steps at a time would wear you out. So, slow down and take a step at a time, and choose to be happy today.

Day 3

Be Positive This Day, Think Only Good Thoughts!

> Finally, brethren, whatsoever things are true, whatsoever things are honest, whatsoever things are just, whatsoever things are pure, whatsoever things are lovely, whatsoever things are of good report; if there be any virtue, and if there be any praise, think on these things.
>
> Philippians 4:8 (KJV)

This reminds you and I what good things we are to think about. Jesus says to think about things that are true, honest, pure, lovely, and whatsoever things are of good report; if there be any virtue, and if there be any praise, think on these things.

So if you are thinking, I'll never get these bills paid, I'll never get my body back in shape, and what am I going to do with my children, Jesus says not to think about these things; only true, honest, and pure thoughts. Turn your worries and concerns over to him; he has bigger shoulders anyway.

Be positive this day, wherever you go and do!

Day 4

That Dream You Have Tucked Away In Your Heart, Don't Give It Up. It Will Happen For You!

> Delight thyself also in the Lord and he shall give thee the desires of thine heart. Commit thy way unto the Lord; trust also in him; and he shall bring it to pass.
>
> Psalm 37:4–5 (KJV)

He will give you the desires of your heart, if you commit your ways unto the Lord and trust in him. I love this verse. I have stood on this verse myself for years. Do you have a dream . . . maybe it's to go back to school, get a better job, or maybe it's to find that special someone. Trust in God and commit your ways to the Lord and he will give you the desires of your heart.

Dreams do come true!

Day 5

The True Beauty Of A Woman Is Not Her Outward Appearance But The Condition Of Her Heart.

When I get down on myself, I enjoy reading the Proverbs 31 woman. I encourage you today, to stop and read this passage, and focus on verse thirty.

> Charm is deceptive, and beauty does not last; but a woman who fears the Lord will be greatly praised.
>
> Proverbs 31:30 (NLT)

It's easy to get caught up in how we look and you can hide a lot with makeup, but you can't hide an unhappy heart.

Every woman can relate to wanting to be their best. You may be a school bus driver or a teacher, a business owner or a professional athlete we all can relate to each other because we all want the same thing. We want to look and feel younger than our age and we want that amazing eye cream that will remove our crows feet. This is what we want as a woman but, god desires for us more than anything, above outward beauty, is a heart relationship with him. He wants you and I to need him daily and to be able to call him our Lord and Savior. This to him is true beauty. So my question today to you is do you call him your Lord and Savior and do you have a heart relationship with him?

Peaceful Reflections

Heavenly Father, thank you for this new day that you have given me to serve you and be a blessing to others.

Thank you, Father, for putting in me special qualities that no one else has, to be of help to people who needs me.

Father, help me to stay positive today and only think on things that are true, honest, purc and lovely. Help me to be the person you have created me to be and to have a heart dedicated only to you.

I love you, Jesus, and I thank you for loving me.

Day 6

Does Your Actions Support Your Words?

Are you a person who says one thing and acts another way? Your words and actions do not match up.

I am reminded of Jesus in the New Testament when He refers to the Pharisees. They thought they could do no wrong, but these men were so far from the truth. I like to refer to this action as a "fake." You talk a good game, but you don't live up to it.

So, today's thought of the day makes you think, *Am I real or fake?* It's a wake up call; search your soul, and make it right.

Day 7

Yes I Can!

Remember when you were a small child and your little playmate would say, "You can't do it," and you would say back, "Oh, yes I can"? We need to still have that attitude as an adult.

As children, we were fearless and somehow, becoming adults, we lose that. I personally won every fight over the bad guys with my superpowers. I miss my superpowers, and I know you do, too.

We can still have those superpowers; the only difference now is the power comes from God. When your mind is saying you can't drop any weight, you say, "Yes, I can." When your mind says you will never get married or find that perfect career, you say, "Yes I can."

> I can do all things through Christ which strengthens me.
>
> Philippians 4:13 (KJV)

This is going to be a good day for you, because your answer for everything negative today is, "Yes, I can!"

Day 8

Nothing Can Stop Me Now!

> The Lord is my rock, my fortress, and my savior; my God is my rock, in whom I find protection. He is my shield, the power that saves me, and my place of safety.
>
> Psalm 18:2 (NLT)

Wow! What a verse, how powerful. Nothing can stop you when you have a rock, a fortress, and a savior. How could you not want to be a Christian? When you are not born again, you have nothing to stand on. No one to pray and talk to, and you don't have eternal life.

This gives you something to think about today. When you have God on your side, you have the ultimate protection, and there truly is no stopping you now!

Day 9

Look Out Dreams, Here I Come!

> For the Lord God is our sun and shield. He gives us grace and glory. The Lord will withhold no good thing from those who do what is right.
>
> Psalm 84:11 (NLT)

> Therefore I say to you, whatever things you ask when you pray, believe that you receive them, and you will have them.
>
> Mark 11:24 (NKJV)

If you feel a stirring in your heart to do something, do it! Here are two verses you can stand and hold onto.

Dreams are a good thing; I have been a dreamer all my life, and I have seen many come to pass. In fact, you are holding one of my dreams right now, this book. God is no respecter of persons; what he'll do for me, he'll do for you.

Don't give up until you see all your dreams come true.

Day 10

I Am Special!

I love Psalm 139. Anytime you get down on yourself and you start to feel less than, read this chapter. Two of my favorite verses in this passage are verses 17 and 18.

> How precious are your thoughts about me, O God. They cannot be numbered! I can't even count them; they outnumber the grains of sand! And when I wake up, you are still with me!
>
> Psalm 139:17–18 (NLT)

Have you ever taken a walk on the beach and got sand in your shoes? The next time you go, pick up some sand and just try to count the grains that you are holding. That will give you a picture of God's thoughts toward you. He is so amazing, and you are so special to him. There is no one else in this world like you. Even twins are not just alike. You are his masterpiece.

So, as you go though out your day today, keep a smile on your face, and know you are special!

Peaceful Reflections

My Father, you are my rock, my fortress, my hiding place, and most of all, you are my Savior.

I thank you that I have a place to run to in my time of need, and that you take the time to listen to me.

Thank you, Father, for showing me that, "Yes, I can do all things through you."

I am so grateful that according to your Word that is the living truth, that you with hold no good thing from those who do what is right.

Thank you for meeting every one of my needs and needs that I don't even know about yet.

You are my Lord and Savior, and in you I put all my trust.

I love you, my Jesus!

Day 11

Look Mom, No Hands!

As small children, we all showed off and tried to impress our parents and friends with stunts we just learned. I myself was thrilled when I learned how to do a cartwheel; when I accomplished two in a row, all of Connersville knew it.

We all wanted our parents' approval and acceptance.

With God as our heavenly Father, we never had to do one cartwheel to get his love or acceptance. You never have to work at being good enough for him. His love is unconditional, and it never changes. In fact, John 3:16 shows how much God loves us. He sent his only son to die for you and I, so that we can have eternal life through him. That is love and acceptance that you didn't even have to work for.

If you have never accepted this eternal love, don't go any further; do it now. Accept God's love for you, and make him your Savior today.

Day 12

I Am Going To Make It!

What a way to start out your day. When your feet hit the floor say out loud, "I am going to make it!"

The first words out of your spirit can make or break your day. Plus, you are setting the tone for your day ahead of time.

If you are sick in body or you have a loved one sick in body, just know you are going to make it. Here are two of my very favorite verses.

> Fear not, for I am with you; Be not dismayed, for I am your God. I will strengthen you, Yes, I will help you, I will uphold you with My righteous right hand.
>
> Isaiah 41:10 (NKJV)

> When you pass through the waters, I will be with you; And through the rivers, they shall not overflow you. When you walk through the fire, you shall not be burned, Nor shall the flame scorch you.
>
> Isaiah 43:2 (NKJV)

That makes you want to stand up and shout and say, "I am going to make it!"

Day 13

Look For God's Best Today!

One of the very first verses I learned when I was a small child was Matthew 7:7–8.

> Ask, and it will be given to you; seek, and you will find; knock, and it will be opened to you. For everyone who asks receives, and he who seeks finds, and to him who knocks it will be opened.
>
> Matthew 7:7–8 (NKJV)

God is saying for us to do three things: ask, seek, and knock.

We have a right to ask him for blessings on our day and on our family. Then seek them, look for God to do it once you ask of him, and when you do have something great happen, give him the praise for it. God then says knock and it will be opened; in other words, it will happen; just look for it and expect it, his wonderful blessings.

Look for them today!

Day 14

Hold Your Head Up High!

> Don't be afraid, for I am with you. Don't be discouraged, for I am your God. I will strengthen you and help you. I will hold you up with my victorious right hand.
>
> Isaiah 41:10 (NLT)

When you read these words, it's not hard to hold your head up at all. You suddenly find confidence and strength you never thought you had. If you are going through a struggle right now, turn it over to God, and lay it in his victorious right hand. He is telling you not to be afraid, not to be discouraged, and he will strengthen you. That is a promise from the Most High God.

So, hold your head up high today, and walk in the peace that he desires for you.

Day 15

Forget Yesterday; Today Is A New Day!

Have you ever had a day that you thought just would never end? Praise God that they do. Those are the kind of days that you can't wait to go to bed, because you get a new fresh day when you wake up.

In Matthew 6:34, Jesus tells us not to think about tomorrow, because it will take care of itself, which is great, because living one day at a time can be hard enough.

So, if it's a tough day, God will help you get through it. Then God will give you a fresh, new day after you have rested your mind and body, and you are ready to be the winner that you are.

Peaceful Reflections

Thank you, Father, for this new day. Thank you for forgiving my sins of yesterday and giving me a clean fresh start to this new day.

You are beautiful and amazing, and I praise you for all you have done for me and my family.

I thank you that I can hold my head up strong, for I know you fight all my battles for me. I rest at night, knowing that if God before me, who dare to be against me?

You are my mighty God, and I will praise you all the days of my life.

Day 16

Forget Your Past, Focus On Your future!

As I set here at my desk and look out my window, I am reminded of my past. I like to reflect where I was ten years ago, to see just what God has done for me. He is so amazing. Your life changes so slowly and gently, you don't even realize that you are being molded and shaped into a new person.

> Therefore, if anyone is in Christ, he is a new creation; old things have passed away; behold, all things have become new.
>
> 2 Corinthians 5:17 (NKJV)

Praise God, old things have passed away. If you are born again, you are a new creation. You have been given a clean slate, a new book with no pictures or words. Now it is up to you to fill it with new pictures and new words of your new life and the beauty of God to you.

When the enemy pulls out your old book with the old pictures of your life, you can pull out your new book and say, "That's old news and that has been forgiven; you must leave me alone."

Praise God for new beginnings!

Day 17

Expect God's Best Today!

Are you expecting something today? Perhaps something you ordered in your favorite catalog or maybe a piece of good news in the mail. It's fun to expect something when you know it's coming; you were promised it, be looking for it.

God has a promise for you today, also.

> Beloved, I wish above all things that thou mayest prosper and be in health, even as thy soul prospereth.
>
> 3 John 2 (KJV)

Notice he says "above all things." He has promised a lot in his word; but he says here "above all things," this is what he wishes for you and I, to prosper and be in health, even as our soul prospereth.

This is exciting; he's wishing something good for you and I today, that our soul prospereth. This means in Hebrew that God even wants our inner person to prosper and to grow daily.

So, start expecting the best from God today and you give him your best today also. What a sweet day this will be!

Day 18

Make God Number 1 Today

How many times have you heard this statement? I have at least one hundred times, but do you really know what it means?

God tells us in Exodus 20:5 that he is a jealous God who will not tolerate your affection for any other gods. When looking up the word "jealous" in Hebrew, it means "desire for exclusive relationship."

Do you have an exclusive relationship with God today? Look at it this way; if you are married, would you want your wife or husband to go all day without talking to you? How do you feel when your mate stays busy with "things," but not with you? Are you seeing where I am going with this?

We need an exclusive relationship with our mates, just like God desires exclusive time with us. Don't you love it when you feel like you are number one to your mate? I know I do, just think how God feels when he knows he is number one to you.

Give him the exclusive relationship that he desires from you; tell him how much you love him today.

Day 19

You Are Stronger Today, Than You Were Yesterday!

Two verses come to mind when I think about strength.

> But those who wait on the Lord shall renew their strength; They shall mount up with wings like eagles, They shall run and not be weary, They walk and not faint.
>
> Isaiah 40:31 (NKJV)

> Fear not, for I am with you; Be not dismayed, for I am your God. I will strengthen you, Yes, I will help you, I will uphold you with My righteous right hand.
>
> Isaiah 41:10 (NKJV)

Do you feel like an eagle today or more like a turkey? I have to admit I have my turkey days, but the important thing is not to stay in those turkey days for long.

Have you ever seen an eagle and how majestic they are, and how all other birds don't fly with them? They are bold, strong, and daring animals. God wants you and I to be bold and strong, and he even tells us he will give us strength.

If you are going through a tough time today and it hurts to even breathe, ask God for strength like he says in Isaiah 41:10, and then look for it.

Polish your wings, and start soaring like the eagle you are.

Day 20

Don't Despise The Hard Times. God Knows What He's Doing

Have you ever gone through a test or trial that you thought you would never make it through? I have and you know what, I also grew as a person through that time.

In your life, there will be valleys and mountains. The valleys are where we rest and enjoy our latest victory. The mountains are where we grow and see just what we are made of.

This is a verse I love and cling to during those mountain times.

> When you pass through the waters, I will be with you; And through the rivers, they shall not overflow you. When you walk through the fire, you shall not be burned, Nor shall the flame scorch you.
>
> Isaiah 43:2 (NKJV)

"When you walk through the fire." I myself don't like fire; it's hot and uncomfortable, and I'm happy to know the flame will not scorch me, even though at times I feel like I have been scorched, and I know you feel the same way.

Be happy. God is by your side, and he knows what he's doing. Let him hold your hand when you go up the next mountain.

Peaceful Reflections

Heavenly Father, I rejoice in my heart today, knowing that with every step I take today you are by my side.

You never leave me or forsake me. You know all my thoughts, the good and the bad. Yet, you still love me.

I am choosing this day to put you number one in my life above all else. I want an exclusive relationship with you. I desire to know you like I have never known you before, teach me your ways today.

Thank you for growing me and making me stronger in you.

I love you, my Father.

Day 21

God Is Always Faithful

Faithful; that is a word you don't hear much in this day and age. Can you honestly say you have a friend that is faithful? Is your mate faithful? Are your co-workers faithful?

God is the only person that is truly faithful. We learn in 1 Corinthians 10:13 that God is faithful through trials and temptations. He will never leave you or forsake you. At times, you may feel like God is not paying any attention, he must be busy helping someone else.

He has his own timetable, and his table and ours is totally different. You can read through the Bible, and see for yourself with all the wonderful stories about Job, Moses, Ruth, and Joseph. God is always faithful! He is your only true, faithful friend.

Day 22

In Your Times Of Trouble, Look For The Fourth Man

This is perhaps my favorite thought of the day; it's so powerful and mighty.

I know someone today reading this is in a hard place right now. Perhaps you just lost your job or your mate has decided it's over, or you have been given bad news from your doctor; it's time to look for the fourth man.

In the book of Daniel chapter 3, you will meet three men who deeply loved God and knew that God would rescue them from anything. King Nebuchadnezzar wanted these three men to bow down and worship gold statues that he had made.

These three men would not bow and even went as far as to say, "The God whom we serve is able to save us" (verse 17). This made the king so mad he commanded the blazing furnace to be turned up seven times hotter than usual. It was so hot the flames killed the soldiers who were throwing them into the furnace.

But "suddenly" (verse 24) the king realized that the there were four men in the furnace walking around, and the fourth man "looks like a god" (verse 25). Then the king let them out of the furnace calling them servants of the Most High God (verse 26).

The three men stepped out of the furnace; their hair was not singed, and their clothing was not scorched, and my favorite part, they didn't even smell like smoke (verse 27).

What an awesome God we serve. The soldiers were killed just by putting them in the furnace, but when the fourth man appeared, the three were walking around. So, with what you are going through today, look for the fourth man, God will deliver you, just as he did Shadrach, Meshach, and Abednego.

Read Daniel chapter 3; read it every day if you have to, to keep reminding yourself just how powerful God is.

Every day, look for the fourth man in your life.

Day 23

Do You Have Cracks In Your Foundation?

As you read this title, I am sure you are wondering what I am talking about. I am asking you just how strong are you? Are you as solid as a rock, or are you soft and mushy like sand?

> Anyone who listens to my teaching and follows it is wise, like a person who builds a house on solid rock. Though the rain comes in torrents and the floodwaters rise and the winds beat against that house, it won't collapse because it is built on bedrock. But anyone who hears my teaching and doesn't obey it is foolish, like a person who builds a house on sand. When the rains and floods come and the winds beat against that house, it will collapse with a mighty crash.
>
> Matthew 7:24–27 (NLT)

A wise person builds their house on a rock and when the floods of life come; they are solid and can't be torn down. A foolish person builds on sand and when the floods of life come, they collapse and fall apart.

So, I ask are you a rock solid Christian and fully grounded in God, or are you mushy and soft and fall apart every time a storm comes your way?

Something to think about today!

Day 24

What Are You Expecting Out Of This Day?

Do you wake up in the morning and decide what kind of day you are going to have, or do you let the day tell you what kind of day you will have?

If you start out positive and full of joy, you can keep it all day. But, if you start out negative and in the dumps, your chances don't look good, unless you change your thinking.

In Nehemiah 8:10, we find the joy of the Lord is our strength.

This should be our way of thinking all day. When someone upsets you, the joy of the Lord is your strength. When someone pulls out in front of you, the joy of the Lord is your strength. When someone takes your parking place, the joy of the Lord is your strength. When someone takes the last jelly donut, you better hope the joy of the Lord is your strength. I know this can be difficult, but it is truly up to you what kind of day you will have. Make it a good one!

Day 25

Are You The Pilot Or The Co-Pilot?

I have seen bumper stickers, a license plate, and even a t-shirt that says, "God is my co-pilot." All I can say is God better be your pilot.

He should be your pilot, your driver, and your captain. We need to learn to step aside and give him total control.

A lot of us are guilty of putting him in the co-pilot position and trying to steer our own ship and then wondering what went wrong. If we could just learn to put him as head of our plane, ship or car then we would see just how smoothly things can work out. Yes, we will still have bumps in our road of life, but at least we will have someone powerful and mighty to go through it with us and help us steer the right direction.

Peaceful Reflections

My Lord, I ask you for forgiveness first thing, because I know in my heart I have made you my co-pilot and not my pilot. I need you to be guiding all my steps, and I realize that I need to seek you for all my answers and not others. Thank you for forgiveness.

Father, I need help with my foundation also; I do see cracks starting, and I ask you today for the strength I need to fix all my cracks so I can be a stronger light for you.

Thank you for opening my eyes today and for helping me to get things straight in my life. I love you.

Day 26

Say Something Positive To Everyone You Meet Today

If you want to feel good about yourself today, be a blessing to someone else. Something I enjoy and you may want to try this: when you are standing at the cash register buying your family some food, you say something positive to the cashier. I stand there and find something to compliment them on: hair, watch, a ring, or their smile. They first look at you in shock, but when they get over that, they always smile and you can see a change in their demeanor.

Where I live is a store I so enjoy, and there is this wonderful cashier, I call her "beautiful lady" when I see her, and I always try to go through her lane. Her face is such a delight when she smiles. She is a blessing to me when I see her, and I do my best to leave her with a blessing also. You should try this sometime; it makes you feel so good to leave someone with an encouraging word.

It is the golden rule after all. In Matthew 7:12, we learn to treat others as we would want to be treated. Make it a habit; be a blessing wherever you go. Everybody needs a smile or a pat on the shoulder. Go ahead and make them feel good.

Day 27

Are The Waves Of Life Rocking Your Boat?

> But immediately Jesus spoke to them, saying, Be of good cheer! It is I; do not be afraid.
>
> Matthew 14:27 (NJKV)

Please take a few moments to read the passage in Matthew 14:22–36. This is a good life lesson. When the waves of life is slamming your boat around and the water is splashing your face and you can't breathe because your child just got kicked out of school, your boss screamed all day, and your husband just said, "Meatloaf again?"

Take courage, Jesus is on the way. He knew the disciples were shook up over the storm, so he gave them a sense of security, and he'll do that for you also.

Just reach out your hand to God, and allow him to calm the waves in your life.

Day 28

You Will Overcome!

I am telling you there have been times in my life where I didn't think I would overcome. I thought *If this doesn't end soon, I will give in. I will have to give up; I can't stand it anymore.* I know you have felt the same way.

> These things I have spoken to you, that in Me you may have peace. In the world you will have tribulation; but be of good cheer, I have overcome the world.
>
> John 16:33 (NKJV)

First he tells us we can have peace in him, which is reassuring. Then he says we will have problems; but be happy, because he has already overcome the world. So, he's telling you and I that when we have problems or tests, we will come out of them, because he has already taken care of them.

So, the next test you face, be of good cheer and rest in his peace.

Day 29

Take Three Deep Breaths, Hold Your Head Up High And Walk Out That Door A Winner

If you can learn just one thing from this book you are reading, let it be that you are a winner!

> I can do all things through Christ who strengthens me.
>
> Philippians 4:13 (NKJV)

Notice, he says all things, not some things, he says all things, through Christ, not through yourself, but with God you can do it.

Perhaps you have a dream or a goal, and I hope you do, that you haven't seen come to pass yet; God will strengthen you to do it. Remember, God is the one who puts desires and dreams in our hearts, so he has already equipped you with what you need to get the goal and dream done.

So, before you head out that door this morning, hold your head up high and say, "I am a winner today," and thank God for being by your side wherever you go today. You are a winner!

Day 30

The Son's Going To Shine In The Morning

You would have to agree with me that there is nothing more beautiful than a fresh new day. Early in the morning, the air is clean and the sky is blue and the flowers are singing their praises to God; there is just nothing like it.

One scripture that has meant a lot to me with the passing of my best friend, my mother, is Psalm 30:5.

> For His anger is but for a moment, His favor is for life; Weeping may endure for a night, But joy comes in the morning.
>
> Psalm 30:5 (NKJV)

The nights I cried myself to sleep over missing her and not just her but other heartaches in this life. Friendships that are no longer; your dream job that someone else now has; or that guy that never called you back; or that deal you were working on at work fell though; it all can tear you apart.

Weeping is a way of healing, but God says, "Joy comes in the morning." It is a new day with new promises. In other words, cry if you must, but don't stay there; pick yourself up, and enjoy the joy that comes in the morning.

Peaceful Reflections

Thank you Jesus for making me a winner today.

Thank you that I can do all things through Christ which strengthens me.

Thank you for giving me all my dreams and making it possible that I can see them come to pass.

It is through you that I can hold my head up high and smile and know that everything will work out for my good.

Praise your Holy Name; I love you!

Day 31

You Are Going To Make It All The Way

If you ever need encouragement, read the book of Philippians. Paul wrote the book to the people of Philippi to encourage them in their faith. The verse that blesses me the most is in chapter 3.

> I press on to reach the end of the race and receive the heavenly prize for which God, through Christ Jesus, is calling us.
>
> Philippians 3:14 (NLT)

You can look at this verse several ways. You can look at it as living a Christian life sold out to God and making it into heaven, and you could look at it as finishing the race you are in now.

Say you want to drop some weight; that is a race, a hard race, but this scripture shows you can run the race and you can finish it and you can win the prize of a smaller dress size. You may be in a different race today, but no matter what race you are in, you are going to make it all the way and reach that prize that you are so desperately working hard for.

You are a winner.

Day 32

Never Give Up On The Dream That You Can't Go A Day Without Thinking About!

Honey, if you can't go one day without thinking about your dream or goal, you got to do it. No matter what other people think or what they may say, do it.

I remember back in the day when I got started in radio, people all around me just kept saying I had to go to school for it. I didn't care for school much, and I didn't want to go back; I had to trust God. I believed God would open the doors I needed open. He did, and I walked right through those doors.

When something stays on your mind that much, God has put that desire in you, and he wants you to full fill that dream. We are all here for a reason, and this may be your reason to be here.

Day 33

Be Strong And Determined!

Determination is half the battle. If you don't have it, than you won't have what it is you are aiming for.

Look at Joseph in the Old Testament; sitting there in prison, knowing he belonged in the palace; having the promises of God, he never lost his determination.

What about the man with leprosy in Matthew chapter 8? He was determined to get to Jesus for his healing. If you want something, be determined.

I have to talk about my favorite little guy in Luke 19, Zaccheus. Now he was determined. He was short but never gave up on seeing Jesus. He knew if he could just climb in a tree, he could see Jesus. What are you willing to climb to reach your goal?

Never lose your determination!

Day 34

You Have Come Too Far To Quit Now!

Have you ever wondered what would have happened if Noah would have stopped making the ark? Everyone laughed at the thought of a flood and made fun of him daily. He was determined to finish what God had instructed him to do. A lot of animals and people would have died. He finished what he started, and we should all be thankful he did.

Now we are left with a wonderful story of encouragement for us to keep going, just as Noah did. People may be laughing at you and thinking you are goofy, but you have a determination that is God called to see this thing through. So, keep building your "ark." You have come way to far to quit now.

Day 35

You Are Closer To Your Victory Today Than You Were Yesterday!

> But thanks be to God, who gives us the victory through our Lord Jesus Christ. Therefore, my beloved brethren, be steadfast, immovable, always abounding in the work of the Lord, knowing that your labor is not in vain in the Lord.
>
> 1 Corinthians 15:57–58 (NKJV)

As you can tell, I am a firm believer in goals and dreams. I believe God put us all here to succeed. He wants us to walk in victory and each day we wake up, we are closer to that victory. 1 Corinthians 15:57–58 tells us to be steadfast (firm) and immovable; in other words, to be determined to get your victory.

It could be a new career, your weight loss, raising your children, sealing the deal at work you have been working on, or winning the case that you have been trying to pull together.

Just remember you are closer today than yesterday.

Peaceful Reflections

Heavenly Father, thank you for making me victorious in all that I do.

I remember where you brought me from; I was so lost and on my way to hell, but you reached down and pulled me out of my dark and going nowhere life, and gave me a fresh new start in you.

I have come to far to quit. I know with you all things are possible, and this, too, shall pass.

Thank you, my Jesus, for dying on the cross so that I can have everlasting life. I love and praise your name.

Day 36

Now Is Not The Time To Give Up, Dig Your Heels In And Keep Going.

I am your biggest cheerleader. I always wanted to be a cheerleader in school. I tried when I was in elementary school, but I wasn't flexible enough. I think all little girls want to be a cheerleader. Now I am a cheerleader for God.

I loved doing the thought of the day on the radio everyday. I felt God was using me to reach out and encourage people to never give up. Imagine you are at work, and you are listening to the radio, and the voice on the radio tells you to "Hold on to your dreams and never give them up, you can and will make it." You don't hear that much, and God was using me.

The book you are holding is my dream, and I am making it come to pass. I care if you make it or not. I believe you have what it takes inside to be a success. I believe you are talented, and there is someone who needs what you have.

So dig your heels in, and keep pressing toward the mark.

Day 37

Celebrate The Best In You. Forget the Negative Stuff

It seems like we are surrounded by negativity on TV and in magazines. Everyone seems to focus on what we don't like about ourselves. From weight to wrinkles and our teeth, someone is always reminding us about what we need to work on.

I am here to encourage you to celebrate the best in you; forget the rest. Sure, you maybe overweight, but what about your attitude, your personality? You maybe overweight, but you have a fabulous attitude toward life. I am a firm believer that if you have an outstanding personality, that is what people will remember; they won't see you as overweight. There is something great about you to celebrate. Don't focus on your negatives; celebrate what is fabulous about you.

Day 38

You Are Fabulous Just The Way You Are

Have you told yourself how fabulous you are today? Look in the mirror and say, "I am so fabulous." You are, there is no one else in this world like you.

You are a masterpiece, you are full of talent, and you are a creative person. You need to accept and approve of yourself.

Before God even had our parents picked out, he had an assignment for you. One of my favorite passages in the Bible is Psalm 139. If you ever get down on yourself, just get somewhere quiet and read this passage. I like to read it before I go to bed; it is so beautiful, and it brings such comfort to your soul, and you fall to sleep in God's wonderful peace.

Day 39

Happiness Is In Your Future

> Taste and see that the Lord is good. Oh, the joys of those who take refuge in Him!
>
> Psalm 34:8 (NLT)

> Oh, the joys of those who are kind to the poor! The Lord rescues them when they are in trouble.
>
> Psalm 41:1 (NLT)

> Why am I discouraged? Why is my heart so sad? I will put my hope in God! I will praise him again my Savior and my God!
>
> Psalm 42:11 (NLT)

Hard times do come. If you are alive and have air in your lungs, you will have hard times. However, as you can see in these scriptures, you can have happiness and peace.

In Psalm 34:8, we find God is good, and you will find joy if you take shelter in him. In Psalm 41:1, we see God will rescue us when we are in trouble. Psalm 42:11 says we can have joy if we put our hope in him. When times get tough, that is not the time to run from him, but that is when we need to hold on to him even tighter. Take shelter in him; give the problem to him. Believe he will rescue you in time of trouble.

Day 40

There Is Always Something To Be Thankful For!

It seems like we are so busy these days that we only stop at Thanksgiving to reflect on what we have to be thankful for. I think God wants to hear "Thank you" everyday. As a parent, don't you like to hear "Thank you" from your children or as a couple, don't you like to hear "Thank you" from your mate? I love it when my hubby says, "Thank you, babe, for that delicious supper." He says it almost nightly, which encourages me to keep up the good work. I am spoiled; God blessed me with a super husband; he even helps me with the dishes every night.

Sit down sometime and on paper, write down everything you are thankful for, and you will find out just what an awesome life you have. Trust me; I have done this, and there is plenty to be thankful for.

Peaceful Reflections

Father, I do have so much to praise you for. You are so amazing to me and I do worship you.

I do thank you for life today that I can serve you and talk to you today. I thank you for all that you are doing in my families lives. For saving those who have yet to come to know you.

Thank you for my amazing husband/wife that you blessed me with and for meeting all our needs.

I have so much to be thankful for, because you are so good to me. I love you so much!

Day 41

Fill Your Day With The Things That Bring You Happiness

What makes you happy? Is it going to the park and sitting on a bench and watching your children play? Is it simply taking a walk around your neighborhood and talking to friends? Whatever it is, make sure you fill your day with one or more things that bring you happiness.

You have responsibilities I know; we all do, but don't forget about you. It will release stress and help you relax and feel good about yourself. Even if it's something as simple as going to get ice cream with your honey, and you sit there together in your car and you share a banana split, fill your day with happiness.

Once you put the kids to bed at night, have some quiet time with a good book and a cup of tea. Relax and fill your day with happiness.

Day 42

Someone Needs What You Have To Offer!

This thought goes right along with Psalm 139. God molded you and shaped you in your mother's womb; you have the perfect DNA that God gave you. He gave you special talents and skills that no one else has. Inside of you are blessings that you can pass on to someone else.

You may be a wonderful listener. If this is you, your gift is to listen to people; be a caring ear to them and offer advice that you may have. You may be a card sender. When you hear of a need, you send a card. This is a talent; not everyone thinks of a special card. I love to get cards in the mail, that lets me know that person really cares to go out and get the card and then write a message; this is a wonderful gift.

Everybody has something to offer. Search inside your heart for what you can do for someone today.

Day 43

You Are Here For A Reason, You Are Not A Mistake

I remember when I was in high school, I was with a group of friends, and we were talking about our families. One thing I still remember is one of my friends said, "My mom and dad never planned for me; I was a mistake." I can hear that clearly to this day in my mind, "I was a mistake." You know, she really believed it. She struggled in school with self-esteem; she didn't think she could do anything. Now that I am older, I see her differently. Yes, her mom and dad didn't plan for her, but God sure did. He placed something very special inside of her, and he wanted very much to use her, just like he wants to use you. She may have turned out to be a Sunday school teacher, teaching your children about Jesus or a doctor with knowledge to save a life. All I know is you may have came as a surprise to Mom and Dad, but you didn't to Jesus; he knew all about you.

No one is a mistake!

Day 44

There Is Nothing That Can Change What Makes You Special!

We all have our own personalities; God made us to be different. A lot of times, you will have people that may try and change you, because they think you should be more like them. As much as you may try to change, you can't, because God already downloaded who you were to be in your mother's womb, and that can't be changed.

You can learn to discipline yourself when it comes to exercising or eating right foods and changing some bad habits, but you can't change your makeup (what it is that makes you, you.).

New relationships are good examples. We seem to want to change our boyfriends/girlfriends for some reason. You will find that you can enhance them by teaching them how to dress better and wear their hair in a better style, but you can't change how God made them.

God has the final say when it comes to our DNA. You are the special you that he created.

Day 45

Hold Out A Helping Hand To Someone Today

How long has it been since you helped out someone in need? Do you have an elderly person that lives beside you? How long has it been since you took them a plate of dinner?

It's not hard to do nice things. In fact, Jesus said it like this in Matthew:

> And the King will answer and say to them, Assuredly, I say to you, in as much as you did it to one of the least of these My brethren, you did it to Me.
>
> Matthew 25:40 (NKJV)

So when you do something for someone who needs a little help, you have done it unto God.

If you know of a family that could use some food because their father has been laid off; if you have the means, bless them with some food. Look around; there is someone within arm's reach that has a need that you can answer. Be a blessing to someone today; it will make your heart smile.

Peaceful Reflections

Father my prayer today is that you will allow me to be at the right place at the right time today to be a blessing to someone.

I know that there will be at least one person I can reach out to today. Thank you for blessing me, so I can be a blessing to others.

Use me today to show your love and compassion to a soul who needs you.

I love you, my Lord and Savior.

Day 46

You Are Amazing! Start Seeing Yourself The Way Others See You.

Have you ever had a friend tell you how wonderful you are with your family? How great you are with your kids? Have they ever told you how much they appreciate your friendship? Then you think to yourself, *I'm not that good, what are they thinking, what do they see that I don't see?* Have you had these thoughts?

We should see ourselves like our best friend sees us. Only your closest friend really sees you. I had a close friend once, and I thought she was Wonder Woman; she couldn't do wrong in my eyes. However, she didn't see herself that way at all. Sometimes you should listen to your friends and learn to say "Thank you" when you are paid a complement.

Because you are truly amazing!

Day 47

Every Day, You Are Making A Difference In Someone's Life.

You make a difference because you are a light, the light of the world.

> You are the light of the world, like a city on a hill-top that cannot be hidden. No one lights a lamp and then puts it under a basket. Instead, a lamp is placed on a stand, where it gives light to everyone in the house.
>
> Matthew 5:14–15 (NLT)

This should show you how powerful and how needed you are to the world. The world is a dark place; just watch the news. It needs more lights like you and I to give it hope. You don't turn on a lamp only to cover it up, so don't cover yourself up and hide your light. You may be the only light in your co-worker's life; let it shine ever so brightly.

What about to your family? They need to watch you and how you handle things. Is your light bright or is it dim? Be the light God has intended you to be.

Be proud of your light, and let it shine.

Day 48

Stay Full Of Joy!

> You will show me the path of life; In your presence is fullness of joy; At Your right hand are pleasures forevermore.
>
> Psalm 16:11 (NKJV)

> Be glad in the Lord and rejoice, you righteous; And shout for joy, all you upright in heart!
>
> Psalm 32:11 (NKJV)

> Then he said to them, Go your way, eat the fat, drink the sweet, and send portions to those for whom nothing is prepared; for this day is holy to our Lord. Do not sorrow, for the joy of the Lord is your strength.
>
> Nehemiah 8:10 (NKJV)

I can't say enough about this thought of the day. Nehemiah 8:10 is a verse I quote a lot in my mind all day. Joy in him keeps you going.

If you have head knowledge of God, this won't make any since to you. However, if you have heart knowledge of him, you will understand.

When you are full of joy, anything can come against you, and you quickly think, *The joy of the Lord is my strength, and God will take care of me.*

When you have total confidence in your God to take care of all your needs, you can rest at night, knowing everything will be all right.

Stay in his presence, surround yourself with good music (some praise music), something that encourages your spirit.

Keep him on your mind, and you will find the joy of the Lord is your strength.

Day 49

Choose To Be Happy

This is your choice. You have the power to make this decision on your own.

You can wake up in a bad mood but choose to change that before you even go out the door.

Take yourself to a mirror, and have yourself a pep rally. Look at yourself and say, "Self, you are a child of God, greater is he that is in you then he that is in the world. You can do all things through Christ that strengthens you and you are going to have a great day in the Lord."

See if you don't feel better. I know you will, because when I have a pep rally in my bathroom, I always feel better.

Day 50

Dreams Only Come True When You Take The First Step!

Boy, is this ever true! Take for example me, when I first had the dream to be a DJ. I knew I didn't want to go to a school for training, so I had to knock on several doors until the right one opened. It never would have come to pass for me if I didn't chase after it. So, it's great if you have a dream, but what are you doing to make it come to pass? Is your dream to have your own business? How about to be a nurse or a police officer? Find out what your first step needs to be and go for it.

Make that dream you have been carrying around come to pass. I know you can do it; I believe in you.

Peaceful Reflections

Thank you Lord for your sweet joy that overflows my heart.

Your joy is my strength, and I can't make it one day without your joy.

I do choose this day to be happy and to make others happy around me.

Thank you Father for making all my dreams come true in you.

You are my joy, and I love you!

Day 51

Have You Struck Out In Your Past? Keep Swinging. Your Home Run Could Be Next For You.

When you think of baseball, you think of home runs. You may have to strike out a few times before you hit your first home run, but boy when you do, the crowd goes wild.

That could be you. Don't just sit there, wishing your dreams or goals will come to pass; get up, take the bat in your hand, and go for that home run.

Call or email that person who can help you. Go see them in person if you can. Keep swinging until you get your home run. We are all pulling for you!

Day 52

You Have So Much To Be Proud Of!

How long has it been since you told your children how proud you are of them? How about your mate? You may tell them you love them, which is great; but, to say you are proud of them is different.

When I was a small child, I always felt like I was in competition with my brother. He always did better than I in school and I knew mom and dad was proud of him. Then there was me, always needing help with homework, never hitting the honor roll and I had to wonder were they proud of me also.

So, have you told your children how proud you are of them? It sure would make them feel like a super star and if they had feathers, I am sure they would spread them out with joy.

Tell them today how proud you are of them.

Day 53

If You Want To Change Your World, Change Your Thinking

Are you a glass half-full or half-empty person? One of these has to be you. You are either positive or negative in nature. The Bible talks about this very thing in Proverbs chapter 23.

> For as he thinks in his heart, so is he.
>
> Proverbs 23:7 (NKJV)

How do you see yourself in your heart? Is everything always negative? Do you often say, "Oh well, whatever?" or do you say, "Sure, not a problem." You are a pretty positive person.

You can change your outlook. Ask God to help you see yourself as he sees you, as he sees others. Ask him to help you see things as a molehill and not a mountain.

Seek his help to change your thinking; he will gladly help you, he is for you and your success.

Day 54

Pray About Everything

Have you ever been guilty of jumping to conclusions? When you hear bad news, have you ever said, "Oh my, now what do I do?" You start wringing your hands and pacing the floor. I have done this exact thing, I admit it, but when I calmed down, I realized how foolish I was. The Bible tells us in 1 Thessalonians that we are to just pray about everything.

> Pray without ceasing.
>
> 1 Thessalonians 5:17 (NKJV)

This means in the Greek version "pray constantly." Wouldn't it be great when we get bad news, if we could immediately turn it over to God in prayer? That is what he tells us to do, pray constantly, and no, I don't think he means to get down on your knees in front of other people at the store or wherever you may be and start to pray. Just take a minute and pray about it, and go on about your day.

Day 55

Just Because Of You, Today Is Going To Be A Great Day

You will never know just how many people that you bless in a day. At work, at home or at church you are blessing someone. When I think of this thought of the day, I think about the good Samaritan in Luke 10: 30–37.

A Jewish man on his way to Jericho gets attacked, stripped of his clothes and beat up and left for dead on the side of the road. A priest comes along, sees the man lying on the road and then goes to the other side just so he doesn't have to look at him. Then a temple assistant comes along, he sees the man but passes him by also. Then comes the Samaritan; he takes care of his wounds and then puts him on his donkey and takes him to a inn and continues to care for him.

What a story, his day was better because of the Samaritan. If you were in this situation, what would you do? Would you pass him by or would you care for him? Are you a good Samaritan?

Peaceful Reflections

Father, I realize that I need to change my thinking. My world can be better and I know I play a big part in that change.

Help me Father, to watch the words that come out of my mouth. The words I speak to my husband/wife and how I speak to my children.

Help me to be a positive person and to see things and people thc way you do.

I want to change my world, and I need you to help me do that. Thank you, my Lord.

Day 56

Even When It Is Hard, Try To Keep A Good Attitude

Paul's attitude in Philippians chapter 4 has always been inspiring.

> Not that I was ever in need, for I have learned how to be content with whatever I have. I know how to live on almost nothing or with everything. I have learned the secret of living in every situation, whether it is with a full stomach or empty, with plenty or little. For I can do everything through Christ, who gives me strength.
>
> Philippians 4:11–13 (NLT)

Now that is an attitude. Even when Paul faced hard times he was rock solid, a life we can look up to and strive to be like. Remember you have the power of God in you, and like Paul says in verse 13, you can do all things through Christ who gives you the strength. Don't even try on your own, but with God, you can.

Day 57

You Are More Valuable Than Rubies

As a woman you need to read Proverbs 31, if you need a little pick me up, on just what you are worth as a wife.

> Who can find a virtuous wife? For her worth is far above rubies.
>
> Proverbs 31:10 (NKJV)

Rubies are my favorite stone and if you have ever shopped for a pure ruby, you know just how costly they can be. We are more valuable than a ruby. Go ahead and smile; it does make you feel good. Next time you see a ruby, you can know God sees you as more valuable than a beautiful ruby. Another great verse in this passage is verse 30:

> Charm is deceitful and beauty is passing, But a woman who fears the Lord, she shall be praised.
>
> Proverbs 31:30 (NKJV)

This verse encourages you to get your priorities in order. Respecting the Lord is far better than beauty or charm; they just fade away. A woman who respects God and honors him shall be praised. This is a powerful passage, I pray you take the time to read it and know your worth.

Day 58

If You Belong To God, You Don't Have To Worry About What Path In Life To Take

> I will instruct you and teach you in the way you should go; I will guide you with My eye.
>
> Psalm 32:8 (NKJV)

He guides and directs our steps if we allow him. Every time we do something on our own and don't wait on him, doesn't it come back and bite you? It has me. I find myself thinking, *Why didn't I wait?* You would think I would learn my lesson.

You will also find if you start something without him, you will finish it without him, that's if you even finish. If you wait on him, everything falls into place, and it just goes smoother. He will guide you; just wait on him. It will be worth the wait and if you need patience, pray for it.

Day 59

No Need To Ring Your Hands With Worry, Trust In Your God

Be still, and know that I am God; I will be exalted among the nations, I will be exalted in the earth!

Psalm 46:10 (NKJV)

This is a continuation from yesterday. I never really understood this, "Be still, and know that I am God," until I got closer to him. Have you ever felt the peace of God? Have you ever got alone in a quiet place and spent time with just you and him? Once you do this, this verse will come alive to you.

I have been seeking him about something, and I have prayed and prayed about it. Then I learned to just get quite and dwell in his presence; the answer will be made clear to you. Be still, and know I am God.

When you have been in this place with him, you will find that wringing your hands is a thing of the past, because you have his peace, and there is nothing that compares to his sweet peace.

I encourage you today; get alone with him, and feel his presence in your life.

Day 60

Cast Even The Small Things Upon Him, For He Does Care

> Therefore I say to you, whatever things you ask when you pray, believe that you receive them, and you will have them.
>
> Mark 11:24 (NKJV)

Have you ever prayed for something and it happened, and the first thing out of your mouth is "I can't believe it, it actually happened." According to the Bible, we are to believe it will happen when we pray; if we don't believe it, then they're just words.

God cares about everything you care about, even our pets. When my pets get sick, I hold them in my arms and I pray for them. He made them and he loves them and he hears our prayers.

If you need a new job, or you are looking for a mate, or you are believing for a loved one to come to Jesus, pray and believe; for he is not a God that lies.

Pray and believe!

Peaceful Reflections

Father, I know I fall short in this area; I am quick to worry. Help me to cast all my cares on you.

Even the small things, you care about them. Help me to lean on you more instead of trying to fix things on my own.

Lord, I want to learn how to be still and know that you are God and have that peace in my heart to know you have it all under control. Thank you for loving me this much!

Day 61

What Kind Of Friend Are You?

> A friend is always loyal, and a brother is born to help in time of need.
>
> Proverbs 17:17 (NLT)

This is an important subject. Have you ever thought someone was your friend, only to find out they weren't? It will wound you spiritually and emotionally. You develop a wall around you, stopping anyone from hurting you again. This will ultimately hurt you in the long run. When you put up walls, they can and will steal your life from you.

My mom was blessed with a friendship of fifty-five years with her friend; they were like sisters. They enjoyed their special lunch they would have and yes, shopping time. If you have someone like this, you are richly blessed.

According to the Bible, a friend is always loyal. Through thick and thin, you are by their side. If you are near people talking and they are crushing your friend, then you, as a loyal friend, should step in and protect your friend's name. Joining in on the conversation and then acting like you love your friend would make you a hypocrite.

I have seen this happen, and that kind of friend is not needed. You are better left alone than have a friend like that. If you have a great friend, cherish them. If you need a friend, be friendly, God will send you someone perfect for you. Someone who will lift you up in time of need and will encourage you in the Lord. They will be a perfect match for you.

Day 62

To Gain A Friend, You Must Be Friendly

> There are "friends" who destroy each other, but a real friend sticks closer than a brother.
>
> Proverbs 18:24 (NLT)

I have heard it said that if you want to be desired, you must be desirable. The same applies here; if you want friends, you need to be friendly.

When was the last time someone said "Hi" to you at the grocery store? Here you are going down the same aisle, you make eye contact, but not a word is shared; that amazes me. Whatever happened to saying "Hi," or "Good afternoon"? People just aren't as friendly as they used to be. Have you ever wondered about Jesus; do you think he went around walking by people and not smiling or greeting them? Can you imagine Jesus being like that? I see him as going by people and saying, "Hi," or "Good day."

In Matthew 7:12, we learn to treat other as we would want to be treated. It's not hard to be friendly; it's as simple as a smile. So, if you are looking to expand your friend list, start treating others as you would want to be treated, and you will have more than enough friends.

Day 63

You Are A Friend Of God, And That Is An Honor

> There is no greater love than to lay down one's life for one's friends. You are my friends if you do what I command.
>
> John 15:13–14 (NLT)

There is a song we sing in church that talks about being a friend of God. The song brings joy to your spirit and a smile to your face. What an honor to be called a friend of God.

After all, he created us for fellowship. Think about it; could you go all day without fellowship with other people?

God is a friend who goes everywhere you go, sees everything you do, and is there to talk to twenty-four hours a day. He never leaves your side. We have the thought that he just sits there on the throne ready to strike when we mess up.

God has a funny bone; he loves to laugh, and I am so sure I give him plenty to laugh at. I have a framed picture of Jesus with his head tilted back and he is laughing; it's my favorite picture in my home of him.

We need to see him as a friend; someone you can talk to about anything, not just when you are in trouble but every day, talk to him and tell him how much you love him.

Tell him what he means to you, just as you would want that said to you. Remember, he calls you friend!

Day 64

It Is Okay to Laugh

> A cheerful heart is good medicine, but a broken spirit saps a person's strength.
>
> Proverbs 17:22 (NLT)

A lot of people walk around like they just sucked on a lemon. If you are a Christian, you have the most to be happy about, and you should wear a smile everyday.

I think some people/Christians think it's a sin to laugh. I know of some people who love the Lord and never miss a church service, but I have never seen them smile or laugh even outside of church.

God says a cheerful heart is good medicine; maybe if we laughed more, there would be less sickness. I believe a person can laugh their way out of depression.

Read a funny book or watch a funny show or movie on TV. Try it today; smile at yourself in the mirror, maybe even laugh at yourself.

Laughing does your heart and body good.

Day 65

You Should Be Proud of Your Gray Hair!

This thought is more for fun, so go ahead and have a good laugh.

> Gray hair is a crown of glory; it, is gained by living a godly life.
>
> Proverbs 16:31 (NLT)

> The silver haired head is a crown of glory, If it is found in the way of righteousness.
>
> Proverbs 16:31 (NKJV)

Doesn't this help you see gray hair in a different light? Just think of all the money you could save by not coloring. The Bible calls it a crown of glory. My mom always said I made her turn gray for all the years she was on her knees praying for me. Now I know it was just her crown and not me. When you do think about it, silver hair is beautiful with a shine to it, very crown-like.

Now that I am getting up there in age, my crown is showing, only I have some white in my silver; I like to think of the white as extra diamonds in my crown. Now when you look at yourself in the mirror, thank God for your gorgeous crown.

Peaceful Reflections

Heavenly Father, thank you for calling me your friend.

I pray that you will teach me how to be a good friend; teach me how to get out of my comfort zone to be a friendly person.

I also pray that you will bring the right friends into my life.

The friends that will up lift and encourage me to be all that I can be.

Thank you for your friendship. I am so very thankful that you never leave me and that you understand me, when no one else does. I love you!

Day 66

Go Ahead Eat, Drink, and Enjoy Your Life!

> So I recommend having fun, because there is nothing better for people in this world than to eat, drink and enjoy life. That way they will experience some happiness along with all the hard work God gives them under the sun.
>
> Ecclesiastes 8:15 (NLT)

Ecclesiastes is a book you don't hear too much about. I enjoy reading it; it will open your spiritual eyes. King Solomon wrote the book, the richest and wisest man that ever lived.

What is the meaning of life? We all ask that question; I know I have. Through King Solomon's life, with his many wives, his wealth, and yes, his idolatry, he discovers in the end, the only true answer to be happy is God. A great lesson for all of us to learn that money is nice and it buys nice things, but it doesn't buy your way to heaven.

We are to enjoy life to the fullest, and we should realize life is a true gift from God.

So though all your work and other duties, take time out to eat, drink, and enjoy life.

Day 67

How Is Your Faith Garden Growing?

> So then faith comes by hearing, and hearing by the word of God.
>
> Romans 10:17 (NKJV)

The key word in this scripture is "hearing," not hear. It means you continue to hear, not that you hear once. You have to keep watering, keep hearing the word of God. After all, your plants won't grow if you water them only once; it is a daily watering that makes them grow. Study to know him.

Write down your favorite verses, tuck them in your purse or wallet, during the day pull them out, and keep them fresh in your heart. Then when hard times come, which they will, you will be armed with scripture and you will be strong in faith and you will have peace that God has it under control.

Day 68

A Good Wife Is Your Reward

> Live happily with the woman you love through all the meaningless days of life that God has given you under the sun. The wife God gives you is your reward for all your earthly toil (work).
>
> Ecclesiastes 9:9 (NLT)

I think this verse can go both ways. I like to look at my husband as a reward. I think if all of us as couples looked at each other in this light, perhaps there would be less brake ups and families would stay together. May be fixing a fabulous dinner for your husband or bringing home her favorite flowers once in awhile would be a wonderful way to show how much you cherish each other. May be by watching a game on tv with him and making some popcorn would be nice or while your wife is reading her favorite novel you make her a special cup of tea. There are so many ways to show your mate that they are your reward. Make a special effort once in a while to show them.

It helps you see your husband or wife in a different light. Pray and ask god to show you little ways to make your mate feel special.

Day 69

Whatever You Do, Do It Well

> Whatever you do, do well. For when you go to the grave, there will be no work or planning or knowledge or wisdom.
>
> Ecclesiastes 9:10 (NLT)

Whatever you strive for in this life, do it with all your might. Don't do it halfway, just to get by, do it well.

Would you like to have a pay increase or a promotion? Do the job you are on now to the best of your ability, and God will increase you and promote you.

Are you a stay-at-home mom? Great, be the best stay-at-home mom you can be, and God will overwhelm you with his greatness.

Whatever you do today, do it well!

Day 70

Pray to Be At The Right Place At The Right Time Today

> I have observed something else under the sun. The fastest runner doesn't always win the race, and the strongest warrior doesn't always win the battle. The wise sometimes go hungry, and the skillful are not necessarily wealthy. And those who are educated don't always lead successful lives. It is all decided by chance, by being in the right place at the right time.
>
> Ecclesiastes 9:11 (NLT)

This is a prayer I pray every day of my life: "Lord, let me be at the right place at the right time; don't let me miss a thing from you." I have never seen such a true verse. The part about the wise sometimes go hungry is true. I once was a part of feeding the homeless and ran across a professor, just down on his luck, a brilliant man who just hit some hard times. It could happen to anyone, and I have seen college students study one subject and when they graduate, they don't even go that direction.

King Solomon was right in this verse. I believe if you pray and ask God to allow you to be at the right place at the right time, you just can't go wrong. He will guide your steps, if you submit your ways to him.

Peaceful Reflections

Heavenly Father, thank you for keeping me and my family safe throughout the night. Thank you also for this new, glorious day.

I pray that you will allow me and my family to be at the right place, at the right time today. We don't want to miss a thing that you have for us.

Also, I don't want to miss blessing someone that you have put in my path. I praise you for directing our steps today.

I give you thanks also for good health in everyone of our bodies. We give you praise. I love you!

Day 71

Refuse To Worry And Stay Healthy

> So refuse to worry, and keep your body healthy. But remember that youth, with a whole life before you, is meaningless.
>
> Ecclesiastes 11:10 (NLT)

We all have been told what worry does to our bodies. High blood pressure, heart problems, and the list goes on when we worry. If we could once and for all cast our cares on God and believe with all our hearts that he will take care of us, we would have to go to the doctor a lot less.

I know it's not always easy; we feel like we need to help God out by worrying. I know I have been there. What it comes down to is, do you believe the Word of God or not?

This is what faith is all about, believing something that you don't see yet, but you still believe, just like the farmer who plants a field. He goes out one week after planting and sees nothing, but he doesn't give up; he still believes he will have a crop. He's planted before and seen results, so he believes he will see results again, if he doesn't give up. So, stop worrying, and you will be happy to see just how much healthier you can be.

Day 72

God Will Have The Last Word

> God will judge us for everything we do, including every secret thing, whether good or bad.
>
> Ecclesiastes 12:14 (NLT)

You can live a picture perfect life in front of people, but behind closed doors, those secrets you think are just your secrets; think again, God sees even those.

If you are hurting your loved ones verbally or physically, and you think you are getting away with it, you may be for now, but not for long; God will have the last word.

Nothing is a secret; don't kid yourself. Come clean daily; ask for forgiveness of sins daily.

> If we confess our sins, he is faithful and just to forgive us our sins, and to cleanse us from all unrighteousness.
>
> 1 John 1:9 (KJV)

This is a promise. We will mess things up, and we will say and do things that are wrong because we are human, but thank goodness he will forgive us and give us a clean slate to start from every time we ask.

I encourage you today; get everything right with God.

Day 73

You Don't Have To Fight Your Battles Alone

> With him is an arm of flesh; but with us is the Lord our God, to help us and to fight our battles. And the people were strengthened by the words of Hezekiah king of Judah.
>
> 2 Chronicles 32:8 (NKJV)

> And he said, Listen, all you of Judah and you inhabitants of Jerusalem, and you, King Jehoshaphat! Thus says the Lord to you: Do not be afraid nor dismayed because of this great multitude, for the battles is not yours, but God's.
>
> 2 Chronicles 20:15 (NKJV)

We all have our battles that we deal with. For some, it may be addiction to drugs or caffeine. Maybe it is a disease that you battle or diabetes. You don't have to walk it alone. The Lord our God is here to help us and to fight our battles.

We have to lean on him and trust him that everything will be fine. Find a Bible verse, one that speaks to you, one you can stand on, and quote it everyday. You can even use one of these in 2 Chronicles about him helping you and I with our battles; quote it and stand on it. Another great verse is in Isaiah:

> But He was wounded for our transgressions, He was bruised for our iniquities; The chastisement for our peace was upon Him, and by His stripes we are healed.
>
> Isaiah 53:5 (NKJV)

This is a good one to stand on. Quote it every day, and remember, we don't fight our battles alone.

Day 74

Are You Fully Clothed In Your Battle Gear?

Ephesians 6:11–17 shows us what our gear is made up of:

1. Verse 14 your loins girt about with truth
2. Verse 14 having the breast plate of righteousness
3. Verse 15 your feet shod with the preparation of the gospel of peace
4. Verse 16 above all the shield of faith
5. Verse 17 helmet of salvation
6. Verse 17 sword of the spirit which is the word of God

I encourage you to read all the scriptures on the armor of God. When I read this passage, I visualize myself in all of this gear, and when I do I feel like I am going to make it, I am strong in the Lord and in the power of his might.

When you are a warrior, you have to have protection and God shares that with us in this passage. Read it like a prayer, and put on your battle gear.

Day 75

You Were Born To Be Successful

> And he shall be like a tree planted by the rivers of water, that bringeth forth his fruit in his season; his leaf also shall not wither; and whatsoever he doeth shall prosper.
>
> Psalm 1:3 (KJV)

> Only be thou strong and very courageous, that thou mayest observe to do according to all the law, which Moses my servant commanded thee: turn not from it to the right hand or to the left, that thou mayest prosper whithersoever thou goest.
>
> Joshua 1:7 (KJV)

These are two very good verses that show us that God wants us to prosper. He has only good things in mind for you and I. I know sometimes it looks like that only certain people get all the breaks, but that would be saying God's a liar, and that can't be true. He knew you before you were even born.

> You watched me as I was being formed in utter seclusion, as I was woven together in the dark of the womb.
>
> Psalm 139:15 (NLT)

He cares about you so much he started watching over you from the start.

You are here for a reason: to be successful in all you do and to be a blessing to someone. Believe it or not, your neighbor needs you; that co-worker needs you.

Put God first in all you do, and he will make you successful. I am not saying he will make you rich, because money isn't what makes you successful. He will bless you so you can bless others.

Peaceful Reflections

What a mighty God you are. You are my Lord and Savior and I praise your name.

Father, as I get ready for my new day I put on the whole armor of God. I put on my helmet of salvation, my loins are girt about with truth. I have my breastplate of righteousness and my feet are shod with the preparation of the gospel of peace. I have my shield of faith and the sword of the spirit which is the word of God. Thank you Father for your armor that you desire your children to wear for protection over the enemy. I love you!

Day 76

There Is No Place Like Being In The Arms Of God

God is a loving God. There are pictures of him hugging children and adults in every Christian bookstore. As a parent, you love to hug your children and as a couple, hugging is nice. We even love to hug our pets. I have six cats, and I love to hug on them; they know when you are loving on them.

God is the same way. When you are overwhelmed with the pressures of life, God just wants you to rest in his arms. Imagine yourself talking to him and sharing how you feel, and he wraps his loving arms around you. You can feel his peace and comfort.

I have even gone as far as when I'm praying, and I feel like this is it; I've had enough. I ask him to just wrap his arms around me and comfort me. He always does, and I feel so relaxed and at peace. You have to learn to look at him as your heavenly Father. There is just something about a hug!

Day 77

Do You Have A Happy Place That You Escape To?

My happy place is my living room. We watch TV in our family room and entertain our guests there, but my living room is mine.

It's a beach room. Every wall has an island picture on it, large oversized pictures to really capture the moment. I have a palm tree with lights that is just beautiful at night. I have pillows on both sofas that are island-related. I even have two beach balls and beach towels and flip-flops in the room. It is a lot of fun, and it's my happy place. I go in there when I need to escape and go to the beach.

You need a happy place; somewhere you can just be you. The kids are in bed and it's quiet; now is your time. May be you can't do up a room, but you can still let your mind escape.

Maybe reflect on a vacation you would love to take. Get out your pictures of your last vacation, and let your mind go back to how much fun you and your family had. It is so important to rest your mind; it is good for your health.

Find your happy place, and visit often. Relax and be yourself.

Day 78

This Is Definitely A Red Lipstick Day

Every female will relate to this. Have you ever woken up in the morning and felt so good and so powerful? This is what I call a "red lipstick day."

Red lipstick makes you feel so beautiful and powerful; it's my personal favorite. Along with the red lipstick, you also throw on your favorite outfit and girl, there is no stopping you today; look out world.

You know what else I have noticed is everywhere you go that day, people always compliment you. Every lady needs a "red lipstick day."

If you are saying to yourself right now, "I've never worn red lipstick before," you are missing out. Find your shade, there are all kinds and put it on; fluff up your hair and look out for a great day.

Try it; I dare you!

Day 79

I Can't Imagine That

Have you ever caught yourself saying, "I can't imagine that." For example, you're driving down the road and see a beautiful home; the first thing you say is "I can't imagine living in a home like that." Or you see a sharp car and say, "I can't imagine driving something so nice." Well, there's a good chance you never will.

In Proverbs 18:21, we learn that the power of life and death is in the tongue. You speak either life or death every time you open your mouth. If you are praying for a nice car or home, and then you say "I can't imagine living in that nice of a home," you just undid your prayer. It would be much better to say, "Thank you Jesus for my nice car or home." Don't undo what you are praying and believing for.

If your dream is to have a grand home, then believe it; picture yourself living in one, plant your seeds of faith. Don't go around pulling up your seeds with your words.

Day 80

Stop What You Are Doing And Tell Jesus You Love Him

We live in a drive-thru kind of lifestyle these days. We like everything fast, and we want it now. We are rushing the kids here and there and before you know it, the day has come and gone, and you didn't even stop and tell Jesus how much you love him.

You may be saying, "He knows I do; I'm just busy." Keep in mind he created you for fellowship, someone to talk to, and he desires to hear from you everyday.

Even if it is when you are praying for protection over your family in the morning, take a minute and tell him you love him. He loves to hear it as much as we do.

You know how it makes you feel when your mate goes out of their way to show you what you mean to them, whether it's by a love note by the coffee maker or a love note by the curling iron. It's the simple little things that we do that make each other feel so good. Jesus loves to hear from us the same way. Just show him everyday in someway that you love him.

Peaceful Reflections

Father, today is one of those days when I can't find the words to tell you how much you mean to me. Thank you and I love you just doesn't seem enough for all that you have done for me.

You know my heart; you see how I feel. You are the best friend I have ever had, you are the lover of my soul, you are my King of Kings and my Lord of Lords. You are more precious than gold. You are my secret hiding place, my shield and my fortress.

You are the great I AM, and I will serve you all the days of my life. I love you!

Day 81

Don't Be So Busy In Life, That You Don't Have A Life

There are a lot of people that this thought really fits them. You call their home, and they are never there. They are busy doing and doing that they don't take a minute and smell the coffee.

Don't get me wrong, I know you have responsibilities, but you need to enjoy your life also. There is beauty all around you to enjoy, if you will take a minute to do so. Grab a glass of sweet tea, get out your favorite lawn chair, and listen to the birds sing, enjoy the blue skies.

Plant some flowers or a garden, and enjoy the beauty around you. Life is not meant to be all work; enjoy some playtime also.

Day 82

Are You A Busy Body Christian?

I think we all can say we know a "busy body Christian," we even have them in our churches. You know, the kind that comes up to you and says, "I'm only going to share this with you about so and so, so you can pray for them." Sounds familiar, doesn't it? What a pity that this has to go on in the church. According to Paul in 1 Corinthians, it's been going on for years.

> I appeal to you, dear brothers and sisters, by the authority of our Lord Jesus Christ, to live in harmony with each other. Let there be no divisions in the church. Rather, be of one mind, united in thought and purpose.
>
> 1 Corinthians 1:10 (NLT)

There is plenty of backbiting in the world; we don't need it in the church also. We are to be God's examples to the world and live a Christ-like life.

So, if you know a "busy body Christian," pray that God will open their eyes to see what they are doing, so they can get it right with God.

Day 83

Do You Have Mary's Heart Or Martha's Heart?

Jesus and his disciples were on their way to Jerusalem, and they stopped in a village, where Martha welcomed them into her home.

> As Jesus and the disciples continued on their way to Jerusalem, they came to a certain village where a woman named Martha welcomed him into her home. Her sister, Mary, sat at the Lords feet, listening to what he taught. But Martha was distracted by the big dinner she was preparing. She came to Jesus and said, "Lord, doesn't it seem unfair to you that my sister just sits here while I do all the work? Tell her to come and help me." But the Lord said to her, "My dear Martha, you are worried and upset over all these details! There is only one thing worth being concerned about. Mary has discovered it, and it will not be taken away from her."
>
> Luke 10:38–42 (NLT)

I can see Martha's point she wants to do a nice dinner, but if I was entertaining Jesus, I would want to be at his feet; wouldn't you? So, I ask are you Mary or Martha?

Are you to busy with details that you are missing your time with Jesus? Are you Mary and soaking up as much of Jesus as you can? This is good and something to think about as you go about your day today.

Day 84

This Is Your Doctor Calling, And It's Time For Your Heart Scan

> But the Lord said unto Samuel, Look not on his countenance or on the height of his stature: because I have refused him: for the Lord seeth not as man seeth; for man looketh on the outward appearance, but the Lord looketh on the heart.
>
> 1 Samuel 16:7 (KJV)

What is the condition of your heart? Is it full of hatred, envy, or jealousy? Is it full of peace, mercy, and kindness? I am so glad that God doesn't look at our outward appearance. It is bad enough that people do. We look at one another and judge each other on our clothes, our shoes, our hair, and yes, our size. God looks at what really matters, our hearts.

Is your heart sold out to him, or are you lost and on your way to hell, if you were to die? The heart and soul of a human is the most important thing.

Take for example two men; one is poor and has nothing, but he is saved and loves the Lord. The other is rich and can buy anything. However, he is lost and doesn't have Jesus. Which one has the true riches in life? The poor man, for he has something that money can't buy, and that is salvation.

He is the one that gets the good report from the doctor that his heart is in beautiful shape.

What is the condition of your heart today?

Day 85

Only The Strong Can Survive

> But they that wait upon the Lord shall renew their strength; they shall mount up with wings as eagles; they shall run, and not be weary; and they shall walk, and not faint.
>
> Isaiah 40:31 (KJV)

> Fear thou not; for I am with thee: be not dismayed: for I am thy God: I will strengthen thee; yea, I will help thee; yea, I will uphold thee with the right hand of my righteousness.
>
> Isaiah 41:10 (KJV)

These are two of my favorite verses. When you need strength, which is every day, and some days more than others, read these two verses.

You can feel the strength go into your body just reading them. God knew you would have tough times, these times don't surprise him; but it's during these times that you have to know, where do you run?

Do you run to him or to someone who really can't help? You need strength to survive. You go to the source of your strength, your supply house, because you are going to make it through; you have that promise.

Go to him today for strength; ask for a double portion if you need it.

Peaceful Reflections

Dear Heavenly Father,

Early in the morning I will praise your name.

In the heat of the day, I will praise your name.

In the cool of the evening, I will praise your name.

You are always on my mind and it's my joy and my pleasure to lift my eyes to the heavens and worship you.

I love you.

Day 86

When Your Feet Hit The Floor, Lift Your Eyes To The Sky

> My voice shalt thou hear in the morning, O Lord; in the morning will I direct my prayer unto thee, and will look up.
>
> Psalm 5:3 (KJV)

Putting him first place in your life first thing in the morning, you can't go wrong. That sets the tone for your whole day. So during the day when something goes wrong, you will remember your God and his promises, and you will feel a gentle peace sweep over you.

Another thing you will discover is how precious your time is with him in the morning. Everyone is still in bed, and it is just you and him, even if it's for a short time; cherish that sweet peace.

Your day is yours to live, but do add your Creator to it, and see just how successful your life will be.

Day 87

Success And Victory, These Are Two Things God Desires For You

> But thanks be to God, which giveth us the victory through our Lord Jesus Christ.
>
> 1 Corinthians 15:57 (KJV)

> Nay, in all these things we are more than conquerors through Him that loved us.
>
> Romans 8:37 (KJV)

In Romans 8:37, "We are more than conquerors." It could have just said, "We are conquerors." That would have made us feel good, but, he says, "We are more than." Also notice it says, " . . . through him that loved us." Not on our own are we more than conquerors; in other words, we can't do anything without him.

He makes us "more than" because he dwells within us. He makes us successful; it's not in our own power. When you are saved and God is your Lord, then you have the ability to accomplish all he desires for you.

He wants you to be so successful and to live in victory. When situations come about, he wants you to have the victory over them and to continue in his favor and be a success.

You are not a failure. You are a success. You have the victory.

Day 88

Do You Go To Work For A Paycheck Or Do You Go To Work For A Chance To Be A Blessing To Your Co-Workers?

> And whatsoever ye do, do it heartily, as to the Lord, and not unto men.
>
> Colossians 3:23 (KJV)

I remember the first time I saw this verse. I was having a hard time at work at my first job; I was sixteen years old. I came home and told my mom I didn't care for my boss; she was difficult to work with. Mom showed me this verse. She then said, "Sis, look at her as Jesus; do your work like you were reporting to Jesus, you will see work differently."

She was right. I have thought of that so often through out my life. I do look at work as an opportunity to bless others around me. It is more than a paycheck; people need what you have. Going to work is a chance to shine your light to a dark world.

Day 89

Magnify God And Not Your Problems

> O magnify the Lord with me, and let us exalt his name together.
>
> Psalm 34:3 (KJV)

What you talk about the most will multiply. If someone does you wrong and you tell everyone you come across that day about it, the situation has grown out of control. It could have been a tiny thing, but by the time you get done with it, it has gone from a molehill to a mountain. When you settle down and think about it, you will realize it wasn't that bad. You got shook up for nothing, and you destroyed your day over it.

Magnify God instead. Talk about him and his goodness instead; you will see how strong you will feel at the end of the day. Keep his praises on your tongue all day.

Day 90

Remember You Have An Enemy Who Hates You And All That You Stand For. Be Watchful Today And Stand Your Ground

> The thief cometh not, but for to steal, and to kill, and to destroy: I am come that they might have life, and that they might have it more abundantly.
>
> John 10:10 (KJV)

Your enemy is sharp and is deceitful; he will have you down and out before you know what hit you. Look how he deceived Eve in Genesis. He lied to her and convinced her to eat the fruit. I am convinced that a Christian goes around with the enemy on one shoulder and Jesus on the other, whispering in our ears. One says that you are worthless, and the other one says you can do all things.

It is a battle, and that is why we are told to stand guard from the thief. Stay close to God and know his voice and know his word and know what to do when the enemy comes knocking.

Peaceful Reflections

Father, I praise and worship you today for your goodness and your mercies, which are new everyday.

Thank you for the plan of salvation and for writing my name in the Lamb's Book of Life.

I realize that I have an enemy who wants nothing but to destroy me. So, I praise you for your protection over him.

I do receive the abundant life that you have laid out for me according to your word in John 10:10.

Thank you, my Father.

I love you!

Day 91

The Words "Settle For" Are Not In God's Vocabulary

> Therefore I say unto you, What things soever ye desire, when ye pray, believe that ye receive them, and ye shall have them.
>
> Mark 11:24 (KJV)

> For the Lord God is a sun and shield: the Lord will give grace and glory: no good thing will he withhold from them that walk uprightly.
>
> Psalm 84:11 (KJV)

Are you believing God for something at this moment? If you are, be patient, keep standing, and don't settle for anything else. God doesn't want you to settle.

Can you picture God in heaven with his angels and you are praying for a need, and he looks over to one of his angels and says, "Go ahead and give them this instead, they will just have to settle." If he expected you and I to settle, then why would he have said for us to believe that we receive them, and we will have them?

I don't think I would want to serve a God that says one thing and does another. Never settle for something. If you want a certain car or home, then don't settle. Are you looking for a certain quality in a mate? Then don't settle.

Wait for the best!

Day 92

Don't Quit Now, Your Blessing Is Right Around The Corner

> And let us not be weary in well doing: for in due season we shall reap, if we faint not.
>
> Galatians 6:9 (KJV)

There has been several times in my life and I am sure yours also that you almost gave up what you were praying for, and then bam it happened. You were so happy you held on because God answered your prayer.

I would like to encourage you today, hold on a little longer. If we could just see God's timetable when he plans on answering us, it sure would be nice. However, that wouldn't require much faith on our part.

God wants us to grow daily in him and really stretch our faith. So, I am here today just to say hold on, don't quit now, your answer is right around the corner.

Day 93

It Is By Faith In God That We Can Step Out And Not Be Afraid To Fail

The scripture for this thought is found in Hebrews 11:24–39. You will find Paul is teaching all about faith. You will find by faith and through faith through out the chapter. It's only through faith that we can do anything.

It's by faith Noah built the ark in verse 7, that Sara was able to conceive in verse 11, and that Abraham offered up Isaac in verse 17. All the great men and women did all things by faith. Nothing has changed; it is still the same today.

When you step out for God, it is by faith that you do. Jesus Christ is the same yesterday, today, and forever.

You want to do great things for God? Then you have to do so by faith!

Day 94

Do You Have The Spirit Of Caleb?

> But my servant Caleb, because he had another spirit with him, and hath followed me fully, him will I bring into the land whereinto he went; and his seed shall possess it.
>
> Numbers 14:24 (KJV)

I like to refer to this as the "grasshopper story," although it is much more than that. It is a good example of positive and negative thinking.

Caleb goes to the land of Canaan to spy out the land; he sees it is full of giants but believes he can possess it. The other spies come back and told Moses that they were just as grasshoppers to these large men. They wanted the milk and honey and all that went with the Promised Land, but they didn't have the faith to believe they could overcome it.

Joshua and Caleb and a few others did believe. I do encourage you to read Numbers 13, 14, and 15 in your quiet time. This story shows the power of your words, positive or negative. When you speak negative, you get a harvest of fear and unhappiness and positive thinking you get a harvest of joy, success, and lots of wonderful peace.

My prayer is that you have the spirit of Caleb today, the knowing that you can overcome anything!

Day 95

Are You Sowing Seeds Of Life Or Death Today?

> Death and life are in the power of the tongue: and they that love it shall eat the fruit thereof.
>
> Proverbs 18:21 (KJV)

I can't say it enough to watch what words comes out of your mouth. If you as a parent speak negative words to your children, then you can't expect them to be successful. However, if you speak positive words like, "Johnny, I believe you can do anything you put your hands to do." You could watch your child live a successful life. Same with your mate; speak positive encouragement to them, and watch the respect grow between the two of you.

The same with your life; speak positive words over yourself. If you are looking for a job, don't sit around and say you'll never find one; instead, say, "I will have the perfect job and it will meet all my needs and more."

Start speaking positive words today, and watch for changes to take place.

Peaceful Reflections

Father, it is my desire that I do see things as Caleb did when he went to Canaan.

I want to be able to see with positive eyes, I don't want to be negative all the time.

Caleb received the promise land and I want very much to receive all my promises from you.

Help me, I ask, to be more positive and have more faith in you.

I Love You!

Day 96

Give Thanks In All Circumstances

> In everything give thanks: for this is the will of God in Christ Jesus concerning you.
>
> 1 Thessalonians 5:18 (KJV)

It is easy to be thankful when all is going well; not so easy when you feel like your heart is being ripped out. According to the Word of God, we are to give thanks in everything.

It is when we are going through those tough times that we are growing in our faith and as a person, so we are to give thanks for that. You are not thanking him for the tough situation, but you are thanking him for the out come.

Say you get fired from your job. The situation looks dark for you and your family; but then God gives you a better job with better benefits; something to be thankful for. We don't always know why things happen, but they never shock God; he always has the answer.

Instead of getting all uptight, start thanking God for what he is doing. You will be strengthening your faith and growing as a person.

Day 97

Stop Complaining About What You Don't Have And Be Thankful For What You Do Have

> The master was full of praise. Well done, my good and faithful servant. You have been faithful in handling this small amount, so now I will give you many more responsibilities. Let's celebrate together!
>
> Matthew 25:21 (NLT)

Sometimes we have to start out small to prove to God we can handle the bigger things. Be thankful for those small things and have a good attitude about them; your attitude is what God looks at.

If you constantly fuss because you don't have this or that, you probably never will, with that kind of attitude. However, if you are grateful with what you have been given, God will bless you abundantly above and beyond.

> Now unto him that is able to do exceeding abundantly above all that we ask or think, according to the power that worketh in us.
>
> Ephesians 3:20 (KJV)

Look at your life differently today, and look around at what you do have and be thankful.

Day 98

Discipline Yourself To Be Grateful

> Don't copy the behavior and customs of this world, but let God transform you into a new person by changing the way you think. Then you will learn to know God's will for you, which is good and pleasing and perfect.
>
> Romans 12:2 (NLT)

The world feels you have to do whatever feels good; look out for number one. There is not much discipline or gratefulness that goes on in this world. However, in God's world, there is plenty of both. It takes discipline to think of others. When you are tempted to think of your needs, discipline your mind to think that maybe your neighbor is in need and what you can do for them.

Putting others first is God's way of thinking. When you think of others, God will make sure your needs will be met.

It is important to keep a grateful heart. It shows God that you trust him, and it opens his hands to open the windows of blessings on you.

Live gratefully, and think of others over yourself!

Day 99

Are You Ready To Live A Life Without Fear

> For God hath not given us the spirit of fear; but of power, and of love, and of a sound mind.
>
> 2 Timothy 1:7 (KJV)

Fear has always been one of my biggest battles. When I was small, my mom told me I would play in the dark and not be scared, and storms never bothered me either. On one hot, summer day, that all changed. The storm was horrific, and it changed my life forever. To this day, I am scared of storms, and I am not real big on being in the dark.

I admit this thought is as much for myself as it is for you. Fear comes from one place, and that's the enemy. You will not find fear in heaven. God gives us power and love and a sound mind, not fear. The next time you feel fear building up, quote 2 Timothy 1:7; I have, and it works. God doesn't want his children living in fear. He desires us to live in victory.

Fear will also bring on panic attacks and can be the cause of severe illnesses in your body. Don't open your hearts door to fear; don't give the enemy an inch, because he will try for a mile every time.

It is a daily walk with God that makes us strong in him, and it is through him that we can conquer our fears.

Day 100

Don't Be So Quick To Judge

> But the Lord said unto Samuel, Look not on his countenance, or on the height of his stature: because I have refused him: for the Lord seeth not as man seeth; for man looketh on the outward appearance, but the Lord looketh on the heart.
>
> 1 Samuel 16:7 (KJV)

Have you ever thought one way about a person and then when you got to know them, you realized how wrong you were? Ouch! I have, and I could have just kicked myself.

That is the lesson we need to learn in 1 Samuel 16:7: not to look on the outside, but look on the heart. Don't be so quick to judge somebody. They may have tattoos and body piercings all over their body, but be sold out to God and on fire for him.

I remember going to see a huge minister from TV, and this girl about my age at the time was in front of me. She had pink and blue hair and tattoos. When she sang the tears flowed down her face, and you could tell she loved God and was happy to be at this meeting.

Here I was, judging her by her pink and blue hair, which was awful of me, but we all do it, don't we? According to the Word of God, it is wrong. God looks at the heart, and so should we. It is not how we look on the outside that gets us to heaven anyway!

Day 101

It Is Not Good Works That Gets You To Heaven

> God saved you by his grace when you believed. And you can't take credit for this; it is a gift from God. Salvation is not a reward for the good things we have done, so none of us can boast about it. For we are God's masterpiece. He has created us anew in Christ Jesus, so we can do the good things be planned for us long ago.
>
> Ephesians 2:8–10 (NLT)

> Jesus saith unto him, I am the way, the truth, and the life: no man cometh unto the Father, but by me.
>
> John 14:6 (KJV)

I couldn't think of a better way to end this book than the greatest thought of the day ever, and that's about salvation.

Jesus said in John 14:6 there is only one way to get to heaven, and that's through him; it is not by works. It is not by how much money you have and how much you have given away helping others. Doing good things and trying to live a good life don't get you there. The only way to have eternal life is to be born again.

You must confess your sins and acknowledge that Jesus died on the cross for your sins and accept him into your life as your Lord and Savior. It is the easiest thing to do in the world, and yet the most important decision you have to make.

Once you do, shout it from the mountaintops that you are saved and your name is written in the Lamb's Book of Life and you have eternal life through Jesus Christ. There is no greater gift from God then salvation.

If you haven't given your heart to God, then please take care of it this day, you will never be the same.

Peaceful Reflections

This is the most important prayer in this book. This one will change your life and give you a fresh new start. It is the plan of salvation. If you would love to have all your sins forgiven and know that when you die you are going to heaven, to have everlasting life with God, then just say this prayer out loud and you will be saved and on your way to heaven.

Father God, I come to you today a sinner, needing a savior. I believe with all my heart you sent your son to die on the cross for my sins; so, that I can have eternal life with you.

I ask you today to forgive me of all my sins and come into my life and be my Lord and Savior. That from this day on, I am born again and my sins are forgiven and I am a new man in you.

I thank you Lord for salvation and for writing my name in the lambs book of life. I now belong to you. I love you Lord. Amen!

Let me be the first person to welcome you to the family of God. You are now my brother or sister in the Lord. Isn't it great to know that when you die you are going to heaven to have everlasting life with Jesus?

What the next step is: you need to find you a good church, a Bible-believing church that can teach you and guide you. I am so excited for you! This is a new day and a fresh new start for you, and all of heaven is singing for joy.

I am so glad you picked up this book. Read it over and over. Get yourself a Bible; start reading it, and watch yourself grow in the Lord. Your Bible will become the most precious thing to you.

Welcome to the family of God!

I love you my Brother/Sister!

About The Author

I was born in beautiful Connersville, Indiana, January 23, 1969 to Junior and Vernita.

They raised me and my brother in church from birth. Every night we came together and read a Bible story and dad and mom would end our day with a prayer. Memories that today I cherish. I am the person I am today because of two wonderful parents.

Growing up I listened to Christian music, but on the weekends dad and mom loved to listen to hot wax weekends with Wolf Man Jack. I paid close attention to the Wolf Man. He always made me laugh and feel good. I wanted to be a DJ. I wanted to help others feel happy.

When I got older we lived in the New Castle area and I enjoyed going to the local park and setting by the pond with the ducks. It was there on a cool summer evening I told God I wasn't leaving until he showed me what my purpose in this life was. Serving him and helping others, is what I wanted to do. It wasn't long till he showed me and I wrote it down in a yellow notebook. He said "What I have called you to do, others can do it; but, not like you." It was years later that I learned it was to be a DJ. The seed was planted as a small child, I wanted to encourage people with my voice.

For years I worked in '50s and '60s radio, did some lite rock and ended up in country. Kicks 96 in Richmond Indiana. God opened my eyes at this station and I started doing "The Thought Of The Day." I didn't get to talk about God and his goodness; but, I got as close as I could. Listener's called daily about my thoughts and what a blessing they were to their day. In 2009 I felt impressed to write a book but didn't know what kind. I told the Lord when the time is right he would show me. You are now holding my dream come true. "Thoughts Of The Day" and I can talk about God and his goodness and I am so thankful you picked up the book.

Each thought is from my heart and a lot of prayer has went into this book. It is my prayer it blesses your socks off and you are encouraged everyday as you read your fresh new thought of the day. God bless you and enjoy it.

—Lisa Collett

In Conclusion

I hope this book has been a real blessing to you. It has blessed me and uplifted me just writing it and knowing someone's life will change forever.

If you prayed the special prayer of salvation at the end, I would love to hear from you. You can reach me at *lmisforyou@yahoo.com* I would love to know how this book blesses your day and just makes life go ever so smoothly.

Thank you for reading this book, and be looking for part two!

In his love and mine,
Lisa Collett